KU-778-914

CONTENTS

What do you get if you cross a T. rex and a hungry piranha? I don't know, but I'd definitely run away from it!

Dive in headfirst to find hundreds more laughs like this. The six sensational, snigger-tastic sections are packed full of chuckles and groans to share with your loved ones, or to keep you giggling to yourself at night.

So, next time your friends all moan that there's no wi-fi, keep them entertained with the most hee-larious jokes on the planet.

CHAPTER 1
In the kitchen

Why did the baker work late?

Because she needed the dough!

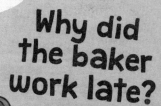

5

Which beverage do ninjas enjoy?
Kara-tea!

What did the plate say to the bowl?
"Dinner is on me!"

What do you call a gingerbread man with a degree?
A SMART COOKIE!

Did you hear about the banana that went to charm school?
He turned into a real smoothie!

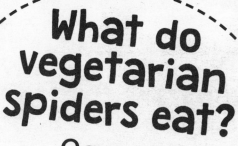

What do vegetarian spiders eat?

Corn on the cobweb.

What did the cucumber say to the carrot?

"Want to go for a dip?"

Where's the best place to keep pizza?

In your stomach!

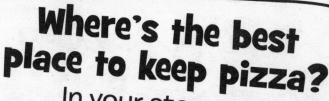

Which pizza topping do aardvarks like best?

Ant-chovies!

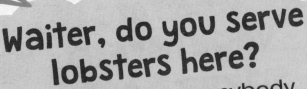
Waiter, do you serve lobsters here?

Yes, sir, we serve anybody.

Waiter, I can't eat this food. Please call the manager.

It's no use, he can't eat it either.

Waiter, what's this?

It's bean soup, sir.
I don't care what it's been! what is it now?

Waiter, there's a snail in my salad!

That's ok, it won't eat much.

8

Waiter, is there pizza on the menu?
No, I wiped it off.

Waiter, will my pizza be long?
No, it will be round.

Waiter, this bread is stale!
It wasn't last week.

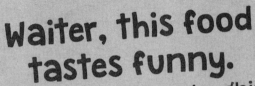

Waiter, this food tastes funny.
Then why aren't you laughing?

9

Why won't you starve on a desert island?
Because of the sand which is there!

How do you make golden soup?
Put 24 carrots in it!

What do you get if you cross three ducks and some cheddar?
Cheese quackers!

Why did the man eat lunch at the bank?
He loved rich food!

10

Which vegetable do boy scouts love?

String beans!

What did the baby corn say to its mother?

"Ma, where's popcorn?"

What's the worst thing about being an octopus?

Washing your hands before dinner.

Which part of Swiss cheese is the least fattening?

The holes!

What did the cannibal order at the restaurant?

Pizza with everyone on it.

How do you make a walnut laugh?

Crack it up!

Did you hear about the hilarious banana?

It had the whole fruit bowl in peels of laughter!

What do you get if you cross a snake and an apple tart?

A pie-thon!

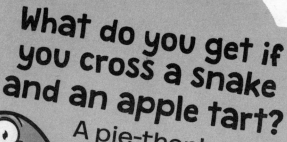

Why couldn't the sesame seed stop cracking jokes?

It was on a roll!

Did you hear about the gravy that giggled?

It was made with laughing stock!

What do astronauts eat out of?

Satellite dishes!

No, seriously, what do astronauts eat from?

Oh, okay then, flying saucers!

Which day of the week do eggs hate?
Fry-day!

How do you make an egg laugh?
Tell it a yolk!

But why shouldn't you tell jokes to eggs?
Because they might crack up!

Did you hear about the egg that loved to play tricks?
It was a practical yolker!

14

Which people like to eat snails?
The ones that don't like fast food!

What did the nut say when it had a cold?
"Cashew!"

What do chimps wear when they're cooking?
Ape-rons!

Why did the banana have to go to the hospital?
Because it wasn't peeling well!

What do you call cheese that belongs to someone else?

Nacho cheese!
(Not your cheese–geddit?!)

Why did the girl love hot chocolate?

Because she was a cocoa-nut!

Why did the grape try not to snore?

It didn't want to wake up the rest of the bunch!

Why did mother grape go on a spa retreat?

She was tired of raisin kids!

What do snowmen eat for breakfast?

Frosted flakes!

What do you get if you mix birdseed with cereal?

Shredded tweet!

What fast food do snowmen prefer?

Ice-burgers!

What did one snowman say to the other?

"Can you smell carrot?"

Waiter, there's a dead fly in my soup!
Sorry, are you a vegetarian?

Waiter, there's an ant in my soup!
I know ... The flies stay away during the winter.

Waiter, there's a twig in my meal!
Just a moment, I'll get the branch manager.

Waiter, why is there fish on my plate of lasagne?
I'm sorry, sir, it doesn't know it's plaice.

Waiter, do you have frogs' legs?
No, I always walk like this.

Waiter, there's a slug in my salad!
Don't worry, we won't charge extra.

Waiter, what's this fly doing in my soup?
It looks like the backstroke, sir.

Waiter, there's something wrong with these eggs.
I'm sorry, but I only laid the table.

How do penguins drink?

Out of a beak-er!

How does a penguin make pancakes?

With its flippers!

What did the penguin order at the Mexican restaurant?

Brrr-itos!

What does a penguin have in its salad?

Iceberg lettuce!

What do you call spaghetti in disguise?
An impasta!

What do you call a peanut in space?
An astronut!

What's the difference between roast chicken and pea soup?
Anyone can roast chicken, but have you ever tried to pee soup?

Why did the chef dream his pillow was roast turkey?
Because they're both full of stuffing!

What do dogs eat at the movies?
Pupcorn!

A cheeseburger walks into a bar and asks for orange juice. The bartender says, "'I'm sorry, we don't serve food here."

Why did the turkey join a band?
He had his own drumsticks!

Why did the girl stare at the carton of juice?
Because it said concentrate.

How do you fix a broken pizza?
With tomato paste!

What can you serve but never eat?
A tennis ball.

What did the vinaigrette say to the refrigerator?
"Close the door, I'm dressing!"

What do you call a really large pumpkin?
A plumpkin!

23

What do computer experts snack on?

Microchips!

Did you hear about the cannibal wedding?

They toasted the bride and groom!

What kind of ice cream do birds like the most?

Chocolate chirrup!

What's red and dangerous?

Shark-infested tomato soup!

CHAPTER 2

Get well soon

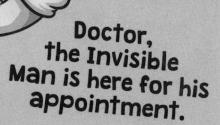

Doctor, the Invisible Man is here for his appointment.

Tell him I can't see him right now.

Did you hear about the dentist who went to the Arctic?

It was a molar expedition!

Why did the deer visit the dentist?

He needed his buck teeth fixed!

Doctor, everything I touch turns to gold!

Don't worry, it's just a gilt complex.

Have you been online to www.conjunctivitis.com?

It's a site for sore eyes!

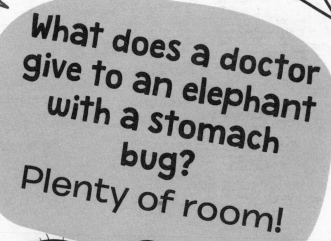

Why did the pie go to the dentist?
It needed a filling!

What's a dentist's top pick at the theme park?
The fluor-ride!

What does a doctor give to an elephant with a stomach bug?
Plenty of room!

27

What do you call a pig with no legs?

A groundhog!

How do you take a pig with no legs to a hospital?

In a hambulance!

What do you call a pig with sunburn?

Bacon!

What did the doctor prescribe for the pig?

Oinkment.

Did you hear about the man who swallowed his money?

The doctor was looking for signs of change.

Did you hear about the girl who was hit in the face by a basketball?

She wondered why it was getting bigger, and then it hit her!

Why are most herbs good at keeping a secret?

Only thyme will tell!

Why did the dentist keep falling asleep?

Because drilling teeth is boring!

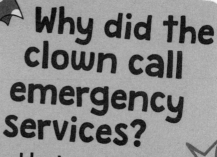

Why did the
clown call
emergency
services?

He broke his
funny bone!

Doctor, it
hurts when
I go to the
bathroom.

Urine
trouble.

Doctor, I
have no energy.
I can't even walk
down the road
without getting
tired.

It's because
you're wearing
loafers!

Why did the van bounce
down the road?

It was a hiccup truck!

Doctor, I keep eating nuts, bolts, and screws.

That's riveting!

Which blood group do teachers most like?

A+!

A handyman went to the hospital after being hit on the head by some books.

He's only got his shelf to blame.

What can you catch but never throw?

A cold!

Did you hear about the pig that lost its voice?

It was disgruntled!

Did you hear the joke about bad breath?

It stinks!

A man goes to see the doctor. He has a cucumber in one ear, a breadstick in the other ear, and a banana up his nose.

The doctor knows instantly what is wrong—he's not eating properly!

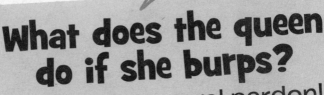

What does the queen do if she burps?

She issues a royal pardon!

32

Did you hear about the frog that had a breakdown?
It got toad away!

Did you hear about the frog that was taken to the psychiatric hospital?
It was hopping mad!

What did the dermatologist say to the frog?
People will learn to love you, warts and all!

What's green and jumpy?
A frog with hiccups!

33

Doctor, would you say I have a split personality?

One at a time, please!

Doctor, I have really bad wind! Do you have anything for it?

Yes—here's a kite!

Doctor, I've got verrucas, an ingrown toenail, a toothache, and halitosis.

Hmm, it sounds like foot and mouth disease.

Doctor, I think I've been put together all wrong!

Why do you think that?

Because my feet smell, and my nose runs!

Doctor, I think I'm a bell. What should I do?

Take these tablets, and if nothing changes, give me a ring!

Doctor, will this cream get rid of all my blotches?

Well, I don't want to make any rash promises!

Doctor, I keep thinking I'm a horse!

Take one of these pills every four hours, with hay.

Doctor, I really feel like a carrot. What should I do?

Well, don't get in a stew.

What did the doctor pack for her trip to the desert?
A thirst-aid kit!

Doctor, there's a man who urgently needs you to treat scratches all over his body.
What's his name?
Claude!

Did you hear about the man that was hit on the head by an icicle?
It knocked him out cold!

What did the doctor say to the volcano?
"You need to quit smoking!"

What award does the dentist of the year receive?

A little plaque!

Did you hear about the moody dentist?

He was always looking down in the mouth!

What did the dentist say to the golfer?

"I'm afraid you have a hole in one!"

Why did the king visit the dentist?

To get his teeth crowned!

37

Did you hear about the man who swallowed uranium?
He got atomic ache!

If chickenpox are filled with clear fluid, what are catpox filled with
Pus!

What's red and thick?
A blood clot!

What blood group do insects have?
Ab!

When does a doctor get angry?

When she runs out of patients!

Doctor, I keep hearing a ringing sound!

Then answer your phone, dummy.

Why are the tonsils excited?

They've heard the doctor is taking them out on Friday!

Did you hear the joke about the germs?

Don't worry, I don't want you to spread it around!

Doctor, I'm so sorry I'm late, I sprained my ankle on the way here!

That's a lame excuse.

Doctor, I keep comparing things with something else!

Don't panic, it's just analogy.

Doctor, I've lost my memory!

When did that happen?

When did what happen?

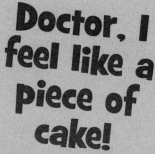

Doctor, I feel like a piece of cake!

Yes, you do look a little crummy.

Doctor, I can't walk properly. I keep jumping everywhere!

Have you been feeling a bit up and down?

Doctor, I keep getting spots before my eyes!

Have you seen a doctor before?

No, just spots.

Doctor, I feel like a cup of tea!

Excellent idea, make me one as well.

Doctor, I keep thinking I'm Mozart!

I'll be with you in a minuet.

What noise did the train make when it had a cold?
Aaaa-choo-choo!

If an athlete suffers from athlete's foot, what does a soldier suffer from?
Missile-toe!

Why did the train worker get an electric shock?
He was the conductor!

Why did the handyman see a psychiatrist?
He had a screw loose!

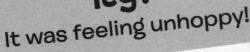

Did you hear about the frog with the broken leg?

It was feeling unhoppy!

What did the doctor give to the bird with a sore throat?

Tweetment!

Why did the snake visit the pharmacist?

It needed some asp-irin!

Why did the duck visit the doctor?

It thought it was quacking up!

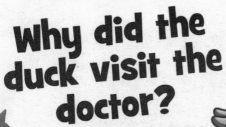

What's the best time to go to the dentist?

Tooth-hurty (2:30)!

What did the dentist say when her plane hit turbulence?

"Brace! Brace!"

What did the judge say to the dentist?

"Do you swear to pull the tooth, the whole tooth, and nothing but the tooth?"

What do dentists call their x-rays?

Tooth pics!

CHAPTER 3
On the farm

What kind of jokes do farmers like best?

Corny ones!

What did the Mexican farmer say to his chicken?

"Oh, lay!"

How does a farmer talk to his animals?

He uses an inter-pet-er.

Farmer Harry: How much straw did you make yesterday?

Farmer Frank: Stacks!

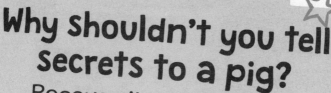

Why shouldn't you tell secrets to a pig?
Because it might squeal!

Why shouldn't you let a pig drive a tractor?
Because it might be a road hog!

What do you call a tale with a twist at the end?
A pigtail!

Why did the pig have vertigo?
It lived in a sty-scraper!

How does a farmer know how many cattle he owns?

He uses a cow-culator!

What does a bull do each night with its phone?

Charges it!

Why do cows have horns?

Because they are moo-sical!

How did the farmer take his cows to market?

In a moo-ving vehicle!

How do chicks save money on their shopping?
They use coop-ons!

Why did the gum cross the road?
It was stuck to the chicken's foot!

Did you hear about the hen that fell into a cement mixer?
It became a brick layer!

Why wouldn't the hen cross the road?
Because it was chicken!

What special deal did the farmer get at the dog breeder's?

Buy one dog, get one flea!

Why did the farmer till his field with a steamroller?

He wanted to grow mashed potatoes!

Why did the cattle farmer move to the North Pole?

To get ice cream!

What do you call a foolish farmer standing in a cowpat?

An in-cow-poop!

What would happen if pigs could fly?

The price of bacon would go up!

Why do farmers choose to keep chickens?

Because they are so hen-tertaining!

What kind of car does a farmer drive?

A corn-vertible!

Why is it easy for chicks to talk?

Because talk is cheep!

51

How do fleas get from one dog to another?
They itch hike!

How does the farm dog get into the house?
Through the labra-door!

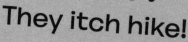

What happened to the sheepdog that raided the cantaloupe field?
It felt melon-collie.

What kind of dog makes you say "Ouch!"?
A Doberman pincher!

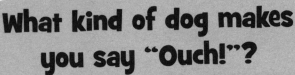

Why did the ram run into the road?

He didn't see the ewe turn!

What did the sheep farmer watch on TV?

A flock-umentary!

What do you call a sheep with no legs?

A cloud!

What do you call a tired farmyard animal?

Ashleep!

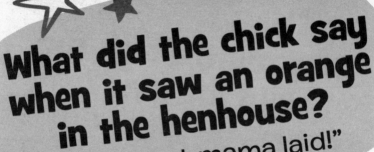

What did the chick say when it saw an orange in the henhouse?

"Look what mama laid!"

Where do you find a chicken with no legs?

Exactly where you left it!

If you had 5 hens, 4 geese, and 6 ducks, what would you have?

Lots of eggs!

Which dance does a duck like best?

The quackstep!

What did the vet say to the goat farmer?

"How are the kids?"

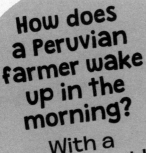

How does a Peruvian farmer wake up in the morning?

With a llama-clock!

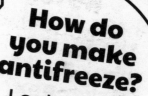

How do you make antifreeze?

Lock her in the barn overnight.

Farmer: How do you hire an extra worker?

Farmer's son: Send him up a ladder?

What do you call a poultry farmer that's afraid of his own livestock?

Chicken!

Did you hear about the farmer who caught chickenpox?

He constantly felt peckish!

What do hens use to tell the time?

A grandfather cluck!

What does a drake wear on important occasions?

A duck-sedo!

Which dog is the fastest over short distances?
A dash-hound!

What's the most used button on a dog's TV remote?
Paws!

Why do dogs run in circles?
Because it's easier than running in triangles!

What did the guard dog say when it found sandpaper in its bed?
"Ruff!"

Why did the farmer send his donkey to college?
Because it was such a smart ass!

Did you hear about the farmer who bred a rooster with a duck?
Now he wakes up at the quack of dawn!

What did the wheat say at harvest time?
"Don't look now, but I think we're being stalked!"

How does a farmer mend his clothes?
With a vegetable patch!

Did you hear about the cat with eight legs?

It was an octo-puss.

What did the farmer call his cat that ate grass?

A lawn meower!

What does a cat have in its bed?

A catter-pillow.

What did the cat say when the farmer stood on its paw?

"Mee-OW!"

What's the difference between an angry rabbit and a fake banknote?

One's a mad bunny, and the other is bad money!

What do you get if you cross a rabbit and fleas?

Bugs bunny!

What do you say to a bunny hitching a ride?

"Come on, hop in!"

Did you hear about the farmer who woke up with a rabbit on her head?

Bad hare day!

Why did the farmer give his mice a bath?
So they were squeaky clean!

What has six eyes but can't see?
Three blind mice!

What do mice do when you're not watching?
Mousework!

Which pet is the most common in many homes?
A carpet!

Which sport do horses play?
Stable tennis!

Did you hear about the pony that ran around the world?

It was a globetrotter!

What did the farmer say when his horse lay down?
"Giddy-up!"

How long should a horse's legs be?
Long enough to reach the ground!

Why was the duck thrown out of the restaurant?
It didn't want to foot the bill!

Why did the vet visit the duck pond?
The farmer thought they were all quacking up!

What's the worst character on a farm?
The robber duck!

How do you catch a unique duck?
Unique up on it!

What did the grub say when its friend got stuck in an apple?

"Worm your way out of that one!"

What has 3 heads, 2 arms, 2 tails, and 8 legs?

A farmer on his horse with a chicken under his arm!

How do dairy farmers help each other?

They cow-operate!

What did the clean dog say to the dirty dog?

"Long time, no flea!"

CHAPTER 4

At School

Why did the firefly get bad exam results?

It wasn't very bright!

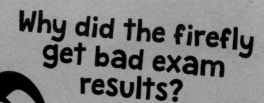

Why was the mathematics textbook miserable? It had too many problems!

Teacher: Sammy, you missed school yesterday, didn't you?

Sammy: Not really!

Why was the broom late for school? It overswept!

Why didn't 4+4 want any dinner? Because it already ate!

Why didn't the nose want to go to school?
It got picked on!

What country do pirates study in geography?
Arrrrgentina!

How do trees get on the internet?
They log in!

What subject do pirates like best?
ArrrrrT!

Why did the teacher jump into the pool?
He wanted to test the water!

What is a polygon?
A dead parrot.

Teacher: what language do they speak in Cuba?

Student: cubic!

Why was the student like a seahorse?
His grades were all below C-level.

Ben: When I grow up, I want to be a school bus driver.

Teacher: Well, I won't stand in your way!

What kind of bus takes you through school, not to school?

A syllabus!

What do you say if your English teacher is crying?

"There, their, they're."

Where do vampire teachers come from?

Teacher draining school!

Teacher: Have you put clean water in the fish tank?

Steve: No, it hasn't drunk the first tankful yet.

Why did the boy eat his homework?

His teacher said it was a piece of cake!

Teacher: Didn't I tell you to stand at the end of the queue?

Jamie: I tried, but there was somebody there already!

Which country do geography teachers like best?

Expla-nation!

Why was the computer science teacher late for work?

He had a hard drive!

Why was the computer thrown out of class?

It went to sleep!

Did you hear about the two IT teachers who got married?

It was love at first site!

What do a cookie and a computer have in common?

They both have chips!

What happened when the baby went to school?

There was a cry-sis!

Teacher: Which was the first animal in space?

Emma: The cow that jumped over the moon?

What's black and white and hard?

A physics test!

Why did the astronaut walk out of class?
It was launch time!

What do pixies learn at school?
The elf-abet!

Why was it so easy for Sherlock Holmes to learn his alphabet?
Because it was L-M-N-try.

Why do pirates struggle to learn their alphabet?
Because they get stuck at C!

Why did the clock get sent out of the classroom?

Because it was tocking too much!

What does the vegetarian teacher say at Sunday school?

"Lettuce pray!"

If sleep is really good for the brain, why won't they allow it in class?

Teacher: Why did you just eat your pencil sharpener?

Jason: I was trying to sharpen my appetite before lunch!

Teacher: What was the Romans' greatest achievement?

Jordan: Learning to speak Latin!

Teacher: When did Caesar reign?

Alicia: I didn't know he rained, I thought it was Hail, Caesar!

Which Roman Emperor suffered from hay fever?

Julius Sneezer!

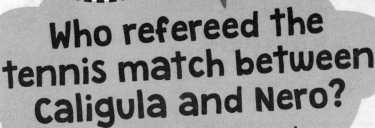

Who refereed the tennis match between Caligula and Nero?

The Roman Umpire!

75

What did the paper say to the pencil?

"Write on!"

Why was the calendar so popular?

It had a lot of dates!

Which hand do you write with?

I don't, I write with a pen!

Did you hear about the pencil with an eraser on each end?

It's pointless!

Which toilet paper do mathematics teachers prefer?

Multi-ply!

Why did the science teacher wear sunglasses?

Because his class was so bright!

Why did the geometry teacher stay at home?

She had sprained her angle!

Teacher: If I had 6 apples in one hand and 8 apples in the other, what would I have?

Sally: Enormous hands, Sir!

Mother: Did you come first in any school subjects?

Daisy: Well, I was first out of the class when the bell rang!

Teacher: Jake, your essay on "My dog" is exactly the same as your sister's.

Jake: I know, Miss. It's the same dog.

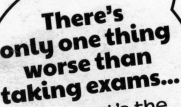

There's only one thing worse than taking exams...

...and that's the grades you get later.

How did the Vikings communicate?

By Norse code!

What did the algebra teacher order for dessert?

Pi!

How did the school cook get an electric shock?

She picked up a currant off the oven!

What kind of cake do you get in the school cafeteria?

A stomach-cake!

What do a burger and a high school teacher have in common?

They're pro-teen!

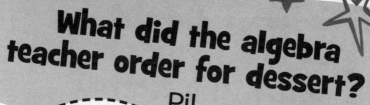

Why did the Archaeopteryx always catch the worm?

Because it was an early bird!

Teacher: Can you name ten dinosaurs?

Mary: Yes, eight T. rexes and two stegosaurus!

Why did the science teacher visit a tanning salon?

Because she was a pale-ontologist!

Did you hear about the archeological dig for elephant bones?

It was a mammoth task!

Why is there lightning in the staff room?

The teachers are mind mapping!

Teacher: Peter, I hope I didn't see you looking at Ryan's exam paper?

Peter: I hope you didn't, either!

Dad: Why are your history grades so low?

Emily: They keep asking about things that happened before I was born!

Ella: what kind of creature is that?

Teacher: It's our pet, Tiny.

Ella: But what animal is it?

Teacher: It's my-newt!

81

What is a butterfly's top subject?
Mothematics!

What is the shortest month?
May—it only has three letters!

Why aren't there any desks in the mathematics classroom?
Because they use times tables!

How did Benjamin Franklin feel when he discovered electricity?
Shocked!

What was carved on a knight's grave if he died in battle?

Rust in peace!

Which of King Arthur's knights invented the round table?

Sir Cumference!

Why were the early days of history called the Dark Ages?

Because there were so many knights!

Why did the cook feed the dragon hot salsa?

He wanted to barbeque some chicken.

Teacher: Anyone who hasn't done their homework will be in big trouble.

Joe: How can we get in trouble for something we didn't do?

Why do all classrooms have bright lights?

Because the pupils are so dim!

Why did the teacher write on the window?

Because she wanted her lesson to be clear.

Why was the skeleton kept back a year?

Because it was a numbskull!

CHAPTER 5
Wild Animals

Why do gorillas have such big nostrils?

Have you seen the size of their fingers?

Why are bears so bad at dancing?

Because they have two left feet!

What do you call a bear with no teeth?

A gummy bear!

What do you call a bear with no ears?

A B!

What socks do bears wear?

They don't—they have bear feet!

How do you start a firefly race?

On your marks, get set, glow!

What toy did the baby snake have?

A rattle!

Did you hear about the elephant that doesn't matter?

It's an irrelephant!

What was the tortoise doing on the road?

About ten inches an hour!

Why did the tiger cheat on its exams?

Because it was a copycat!

What do cheetahs eat?

Fast food!

Why don't cheetahs wash?

They don't want to be spotless!

Where did the leopard have its picnic?

It found just the right spot!

What's the easiest way to catch a fish?

Ask someone to throw it to you!

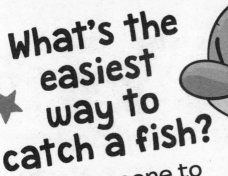

WHY did the whale forgive the dolphin for bumping into it?

Because it didn't do it on porpoise!

What does an octopus wear to keep it warm?

A coat of arms!

Where do sharks go for a break?

Finland!

What did the lion say when the zookeeper stopped it from eating the dictionary?

"You took the words right out of my mouth!"

What happened to the lion that spent Christmas at the beach?

It got sandy claws!

What do you get if you spill birdseed in your shoes?

Pigeon toes!

Why did the lion eat the tightrope walker?

It wanted a well-balanced meal!

What should a lizard do if it loses its tail?

Go to a retail outlet!

Why wouldn't the hyena play cards with the other animals?

Because one was a cheetah, and the other was lion!

What's worse than a bull in a china shop?

A porcupine in a balloon factory!

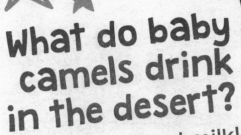

What do baby camels drink in the desert?

Evaporated milk!

What do you get if you cross a parrot and a lion?
A bird that talks your head off!

What's the best time to buy a canary?
When it's going cheep!

Why do seagulls live by the sea?
Because if they lived by the bay, they would be bagels!

What did the macaw say to the toucan?
"Talk is cheep!"

What's black and white and red all over?

A sunburned zebra!

Where do you usually find sloths?

It depends on where you left them!

Why don't anteaters get ill?

Because they're full of anty-bodies!

What's black and white and eats like a horse?

A zebra!

93

What do you call a lion with an upset stomach?

Rory!

What do you call a tiger that has eaten your dad's sister?

An aunt-eater!

What's the difference between a tiger and a lion?

A tiger has the mane part missing!

What day of the week do lions like best?

Chewsday!

What do you get if you cross a herd of elephants with a truckload of prunes?

Out of the way!

What haunts graveyards in Africa?

Elephantoms!

What's brown on the outside and striped in the middle?

A zebra sandwich!

What did the doctor give to the nervous elephant?

Trunkquilizers!

Who won gold at the giraffe Olympics?
Nobody—they were all neck and neck!

What do giraffes have that no other animal has?
Baby giraffes!

Why do giraffes have such long necks?
Because their feet smell!

What's green and slimy and hangs from trees?
Giraffe snot!

What dance did the elephants do in the living room?

Breakdancing!

Did you hear about the cobras who fought?

They eventually hissed and made up!

What weighs a ton and floats gracefully through the air?

A hang-gliding rhinoceros!

Did you hear about the rhino that caught a cold?

It was a rhi-snot-eros!

How do you stop a skunk from smelling?
Hold its nose!

How many skunks does it take to make a really, really bad smell?
A phew!

Why do skunks argue a lot?
Because they like to raise a stink!

What do you call a dead skunk?
Ex-stinked!

What's worse than when it's raining cats and dogs?
Hailing a taxi!

What do seagulls tell their children before bed?
Ferry tales!

What bird jumps out of planes?
A parrot-trooper!

What does a toucan wear to go swimming?
A beak-ini!

99

Why did the polar bear return some food to the store?

Because the seal was broken!

What do you call a man who lives with a pack of wolves?

Wolfgang!

What do polar bears do when they're not hunting?

They just chill!

Did you hear about the stranded polar bear?

It was ice-olated!

What do you call a really, really old ant?

An antique!

What's the best job for a spider?

Web designer!

What do you get if you cross a centipede and a parrot?

A walkie-talkie!

What's the difference between a coyote and a flea?

One howls on the prairie, the other prowls on the hairy!

What's brown and dangerous and lives in a tree?

A monkey with a hand grenade!

Did you hear about the snake that swallowed some keys?

It got lockjaw!

What's large and squirts jam at you?

An elephant eating a donut!

What do you call an alligator that works for the police?

An investi-gator!

What has 99 legs and one eye?

A pirate centipede!

Did you hear about the rich spiders that got married?

They had an elaborate webbing!

What do you call someone who keeps flying squirrels?

A branch manager!

On what day do spiders feel very happy?

Webs-day!

What game do jellyfish play at parties?
Tide-and-seek!

Why did the octopus leave the ocean?
It went to join the army!

How do dolphins decide who goes first?
Flipper coin!

Where do basking sharks keep their belongings?
On the continental shelf!

CHAPTER 6
Monsters and Aliens

What dessert do monsters love best?

Shockolate pudding!

Why did the skull win the race?

Because it was ahead!

How can you tell if a skeleton owns an umbrella?

It's bone dry!

Why can't skeletons play hymns in church?

Because they have no organs!

Who works at a haunted house?

Skeleton staff!

What kind of coffee do vampires drink at night?

Decoffinated!

What's a vampire's top celebration?

Fangs-giving!

Did you hear about the bad-tempered vampire?

He kept flipping his lid!

What kind of blood do pessimistic vampires like best?

B negative!

What did the ghost order at the restaurant?
Ghoulash!

What did the skeleton order at the restaurant?
Spare ribs!

What do skeletons say before each meal?
"Bone appetit!"

Where do sea monsters live?
The dead sea!

Which dessert do ghosts like best?

I-scream!

Why do witches love pork roast?

Because of all the cackling!

What do witches like on their sandwiches?

Scream cheese!

What do monsters eat with their sandwiches?

Human beans!

How do mummies hide?

They wear masking tape!

What do you call a friendly pharaoh?

A chummy mummy!

Why can you trust a mummy with your secrets?

They're good at keeping things under wraps!

What do Egyptian monsters call their parents?

Mummy and Deady!

When does a zombie go to sleep?
When it's dead tired!

Why did the shark vomit after it ate the rector?
Because it's hard to keep a good man down!

What's black and white and dead all over?
A zombie in a tuxedo!

What do you call a werewolf with no money?
Paw!

111

Where do bright aliens study?

Universe-ity!

How do you get a baby alien to sleep?

Rocket!

What do aliens wear at weddings?

Spacesuits!

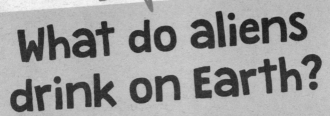

What do aliens drink on Earth?

Gravitea!

What do you call a witch at the seaside?

A sand-witch!

Who saves drowning spooks at the seaside?

The ghostguard!

What do you call a witch at the seaside who is too scared to swim?

A chicken sand-witch!

Did you hear about the witch in the four star hotel?

She ordered broom service!

Where can you buy cheap zombies?

At a monster sale!

What is a zombie most likely to receive a medal for?

Deadication!

Did you hear about the overworked zombie?

He was dead on his feet!

What advice should you remember if you're running away from a zombie?

Don't go down any dead ends!

What do little vampires eat?

Alpha-bat soup!

Did you hear about the vampire who loved baseball?

Each night he turned into a bat!

Why should you be especially afraid of a vampire dog?

Its bite is worse than its bark!

Why did all of Dracula's servants quit?

Because of his bat temper!

Where did the zombie go for a break?
The deaditerranean coast!

Where's the safest place to hide from a zombie?
In the living room!

Where did the zombie go the following year?
Death Valley!

Why didn't the zombie get the job at a summer camp?
They wanted someone more lively!

What do aliens do to congratulate their teammates?

They give each other a high six!

How can you tell if an alien has used your hairbrush?

It glows in the dark!

How can you tell if an alien has used your toothbrush?

It tastes like alien spit!

Where should you send a dirty alien?

Into a meteor shower!

What do elves use to make their sandwiches?
Shortbread!

What directions did the goblin give to the lost ghost?
Go straight on, then make a fright at the corner!

What do you call a sprite with a twisted ankle?
A hobblin' goblin!

Where do baby banshees learn to wail?
In noisery school!

Why was the monster at the top of the class?

Because two heads are better than one!

Who goes to ghost school?

Ghoulboys and ghoulgirls!

Why wouldn't the vampire teacher leave the cafeteria?

She was on her coffin break!

What do zombies play in the playground?

Corpses and robbers!

What shade of clothes do banshees wear?

Yeller!

Who's the worst player on the ghoul soccer team?

The Grim Keeper!

Did you hear about the poltergeist in the china shop?

It had a smashing time!

How did the wizard know the time?

He checked his wrist witch!

What does a monster take for a splitting headache?

Superglue!

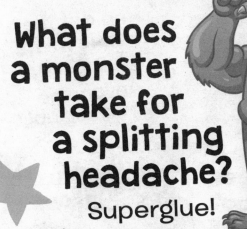

What's big and ugly and blue?

A monster holding its breath!

How do ghosts begin business letters?

"Tomb it may concern ..."

Which monster is good at science?

Frank Einstein!

Which game do zombies like best?
Chase!

Who did the zombie invite to his party? Anyone he could dig up!

What kind of music do mummies enjoy?
Wrap music!

122

What's a swamp monster's top party game?
Stick in the mud!

What's a ghoul's top party game?
Musical scares!

What's a monster's top party game?
Swallow my leader!

What's a ghost's top party game?
Hide-and- shriek!

What's a vampire's top party game?
Sleeping lions!

What kind of ice cream do vampires like best?
Veinilla!

What did the vampire doctor say?
Necks, please!

Which dessert do ghouls like best?
Strawberries and scream!

Why should a mummy be careful when it rests?
So it doesn't unwind too much!

When is it easy to beat a zombie in an argument?

When it has no leg to stand on!

Who won the zombie sprint?

No one, it was a dead heat!

What's a zombie's happy hour?

Ate o'clock!

What does a zombie read first in the newspaper?

Its horrorscope!

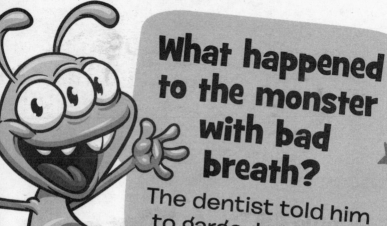

What happened to the monster with bad breath?

The dentist told him to gargoyle twice a day!

Why did the boy throw eggs at the aliens?

He wanted to eggs-terminate them!

What's an alien's top sweet treat?

Martian-mallows!

What do you give to an alien with facial stubble?

A laser blade!

What did the ogre
say when he saw his
friend's monster truck?

"I'm green with envy!"

Grandma ogre:
Did you pick
your nose?

Little ogre:
No, I was born
with it!

What does
an ogre
drive?

A monster
truck!

What did
the daddy
ogre say
to his
son?

"Stop goblin
your food!"

Loopy Library

Spotting a Shooting Star
by Omar Gosh

Tracking UFOs
by Luke Out

Astrophysics
by Jean Yuss

Top 10 Telescopes
by Seymour Stars

The Aliens Are Here!
by Sue Prize

The Edge of the Universe
by Otto Sight

Rocket Launch
by Ivana Blastov

Alien Abduction
by Y. Me

Stargazing
by Wan Tranced

'Be warned, this is not a tale where wrongdoers are punished and the exploited are vindicated. This has nothing to do with the gilded, safe and privileged Georgian era of Jane Austen. History rarely provides a comfortable moral to a good yarn.'